In Memory of

Phyllis Jane Best

Mother

of

Jane Foust

by

Blairsville
Middle School Faculty

OUTDOOR LIFE

essential
GARDENING
for teens

Ruth Chasek

Children's Press
A Division of Grolier Publishing
New York / London / Hong Kong / Sydney
Danbury, Connecticut

To Noah, Naomi, Solitaire,
and to Jane Farwell, whose garden was an inspiration

Book Design: Lisa Quattlebaum
Contributing Editor: Jennifer Ceaser

Photo Credits: pp. 5, 6, 26 by Michelle Edwards; pp. 9, 28, 29 © PhotoDisc; pp. 12, 28, 29 © PhotoDisc; p. 17 © Chris Bartlett/ FPG International; p. 19 © Jim West/Impact Visuals; p. 20 © Scott Barrow/International Stock; p. 22 © Jim Sugar Photography/ Corbis; p. 31 © Patrick Johns/Corbis; p. 32 © Paul Avis/FPG International; p. 35 © George Lepp/Corbis; p. 37 © Ken Wilson, Papilio/Corbis.

Visit Children's Press on the Internet at:
http://publishing.grolier.com

Library of Congress Cataloging-in-Publication Data

Chasek, Ruth.
   Essential gardening for teens / by Ruth Chasek.
      p. cm—(Outdoor life)
   Includes bibliographical references (p. 44) and index.
   Summary: Provides information on planning, preparing, planting, and
      taking care of a garden plot or container garden.
   ISBN 0-516-23356-4 (lib. bdg.)—ISBN 0-516-23556-7 (pbk.)
1. Gardening for teenagers—Juvenile literature. [1. Gardening.] I. Title. II.
      Outdoor life
   (New York, N.Y.)

SB457.4.T44 C53 2000
635—dc21

                                                            99-044797

CONTENTS

Introduction

Long before there were grocery stores and supermarkets, people used to grow food in gardens. Today, many people still choose to grow their own fruits, vegetables, and herbs. A garden where fresh produce is grown is called a kitchen garden. Other people like to have a flowering garden. A flowering garden is made up of flowers and other attractive plants. No matter which kind of plants you choose to grow, you need to provide them three basic things: sun, water, and soil.

This book will help you with planning and planting your garden. It will also offer tips on how to be a great gardener.

Many people like to grow their own produce.

1
Planning Your Garden

It's important to make a plan for your garden before you start planting.

To start your garden you will need a plan. How much space do you have? Will your garden be outdoors or indoors? Will it be in the ground or in containers? Think about what you would like to grow: fruits, vegetables, herbs, flowers, or a little bit of everything? It's important to plan before you plant.

First, you need to decide if you want to grow a garden plot or a container garden. A garden plot is outdoors, in the ground. A container garden can be indoors or outdoors, in containers. Now look carefully at the area that you have to work with. Choose a sunny spot away from trees or bushes that can shade your garden. If you decide to have a garden plot, don't put it near pipes, cables, or anywhere that is unsafe to dig.

Next, find out about each plant before you buy it. You can read the back of the seed packet or check a gardening book. You can also talk with someone who works at your local gardening center, or nursery. Here are some things you will need to research:

• How much space will the full-grown plant need? Some plants require more space to grow than others do. Find out the adult plant's total height and spread (width). For container gardening, be sure you have containers deep enough for the plant's roots to grow.

• How much or how little sun will the plant require? Some plants need full sun. Others prefer some shade. You will need to take into account how much sun your garden gets each day.

• What time of year should the seed, seedling (small, young plant), or bulb (large, swollen seed) be planted? Planting during the right season is important if your garden is going to be outdoors. Some plants can go in the ground in early spring, when it's still cool. Others need to wait for warmer weather. Bulbs may need to be planted six to eight months ahead of time.

Choosing Your Plants

You've determined how much space you'll have in your garden. You also know what size plants you need to buy. Here are some other things to keep in mind when buying your plants:

• Annual plants grow and bloom for one season. Petunias, marigolds, and basil are all annual plants.

• Biennial plants grow and bloom for two seasons. Parsley, poppies, and carnations are biennials.

• Perennial plants come up year after year. Perennials include daffodils, hollyhocks, and chives.

9

MAKING A GARDEN PLAN

It will help to draw a plan of your garden first. A plan will help you to know if there's enough space and sun for the plants that you want to grow. A plan will also help you to arrange your plants in a particular pattern. You may want a pattern if you're growing a flower garden.

Gardening Tip

If you're buying a flowering plant, buy it in full bloom so you can make sure of the flower color.

For container gardening, it helps to map out where the containers are going to be placed. Draw the areas where you will put the plants, such as a windowsill or porch. Determine which areas receive the right amount of sunlight for each type of plant. Then you can figure out how much space you have and how many containers you will need.

Map Out Your Garden

3 feet (91 cm) long

← 4 feet (121 cm) wide →

To map out a garden that is 4 feet wide by 3 feet long (121 cm by 91 cm), draw twelve 1-inch (2 $\frac{1}{2}$-cm) squares on paper. Determine how much space each plant will need. Generally, each plant will need one square foot (77 sq. cm) of growing space. Then indicate where each plant will be placed in the garden. Don't forget to leave room to walk between the rows of plants.

2
Preparing Your Garden

Make sure to have the tools you need before you begin gardening.

Now that you've made your garden plan, it's time to get your garden ready for planting. To prepare your garden, you need to have the right kind of garden tools. You should also add one or more of the following to your soil:

- fertilizer (plant food, such as dried manure)
- compost (decayed plant scraps)
- peat moss (decayed moss)
- vermiculite (a light rock that absorbs water)

Fertilizer and compost make the soil healthy. They give the plants nutrients that may not be found in regular backyard dirt. Peat moss and vermiculite help to keep in moisture and warmth. Plants need moist, warm conditions to grow. You can find these soil helpers at your local garden center.

Tools You Will Need

GARDEN PLOT	CONTAINER GARDEN
spade or shovel (to dig and break up lumps in the soil)	trowel or a large serving spoon (to dig)
metal rake (to smooth the soil's surface)	old fork (to smooth the soil's surface)
watering can or hose	watering can
trowel (a hand-held spade for digging smaller holes)	spray bottle (to mist indoor plants)

GARDENING TOOLS

What tools will you need to buy before you start planting? It depends on whether you'll be working with a garden plot or using containers. No matter the kind of garden, when planting outdoors always wear gardening gloves and a hat with a wide brim.

TO PREPARE A GARDEN PLOT
You will need:

- shovel or spade
- metal rake
- peat moss, compost, or fertilizer
- four wooden or metal stakes
- string or twine
- garden markers

You will want to mark off your garden plot so that no one will accidentally step on your plants. Put a stake at each corner of the plot.

15

Tie string around each marker so that all of the four sides are surrounded. Then prepare the soil. Using a spade or shovel, dig up the soil. Turn it over as you go so that the ground is loosened. Break up any big clumps of dirt. Remove rocks, grass, and other objects. It's a good idea to mix peat moss, compost, or a small amount of fertilizer into the soil. Then use a metal rake to smooth the soil's surface and make it level.

For a kitchen garden, you will probably want to organize your garden in rows. Mark rows with garden markers—one marker at each end. Markers tell you where the rows are and what has been planted in each. Garden markers can be made with Popsicle™ sticks. You also can use paint stirrers (ask at a hardware store) or you can cut strips from plastic containers. Use a pen with permanent ink to write the name of the plants on the markers.

You can grow a container garden in almost anything.

TO PREPARE A CONTAINER GARDEN

You will need:

- potting soil
- peat moss or vermiculite
- scissors
- garden markers
- pebbles or newspaper

Containers can be colorful flowerpots, window boxes, or you can make them yourself. Anything large enough to hold dirt can be used. Containers can be made from gallon-size plastic milk cartons, buckets, or milk crates lined with garbage bags. Just make sure there's enough room for a full-grown plant. Wash your homemade container. Use scissors to poke holes in the bottom for water to drain. Line the bottom with a layer of pebbles or newspaper. Fill the container with potting soil or a mixture of soil, peat moss, and vermiculite. Peat moss and vermiculite are lighter than soil, which will make the containers easier to move. Use markers to indicate what kind of plant is in each container.

COMMUNITY AND CITY GARDENS

Maybe you don't have sun or space for the plants you want to grow. You can still participate by joining a community garden. Community gardens can be found in many places: the country, the suburbs, and especially in big cities. Often neighbors have worked

Community gardens are a great way to get involved in gardening.

together to make a garden out of an empty piece of land. Each person is given a small plot to work. You may be able to share the cost of gardening supplies with other members.

If you notice a community garden in your neighborhood, stop and ask how to join. To find one, call a local botanical garden, public library, or The American Community Garden Association (see page 45). A community garden is a place where you can meet new people. They may know a lot about gardening and can share their knowledge with you.

3
Planting Your Garden

Now that you've prepared the soil, your garden is
ready for planting.

You have chosen the plants you want to grow. You've also prepared the soil. Now it's time to start planting. You'll need to decide whether you want to buy seeds, bulbs, or seedlings. Think about how much money you want to spend and how much work you want to put into your garden. Seedlings are the easiest to grow but can be expensive. Seeds and bulbs are cheaper than seedlings, and it's also fun to watch them sprout and grow.

SEEDS

A seed contains all of the necessary elements to grow into a plant. Its hard coat is like a shell, protecting the living material inside. It's important to plant your seeds correctly—under warm, moist conditions—so that they will sprout.

How to Plant Seeds
You will need:

- trowel, spoon, or stick
- ruler
- seeds

Read the back of the seed packet to see (1) how far apart the seeds should be planted, and (2) how deep the seeds need to be planted. In a garden plot, use a trowel to dig a trench (narrow ditch) down the middle of each row. In a container, use a stick or a spoon to make each hole. With a ruler, measure the depth to check that it is correct. If large seeds are planted too close to the surface, they will dry out. Small seeds won't be able to grow if they are planted too deep in the soil. As a rule, you want to plant seeds about three times as deep as they are wide.

Drop the seeds in the trench or holes, and then cover them with soil. Gently pat the dirt. Don't pack the dirt, or the seeds won't be able to sprout through the hard ground. Water the soil lightly. Too much water will wash away the seeds.

Give Your Seeds a Head Start

You can give your seeds a head start by growing them indoors. When they become seedlings, you can replant them in your garden. You should start seeds indoors if the plant is sensitive to cold weather. You also should do this if the

Gardening Tip

Once you get your garden started, you can begin saving your own seeds from dry flowers picked in the fall.

ground is too cold or hard to plant the seeds.
You will need:

- containers (such as egg cartons,
  paper or plastic cups, yogurt containers, tin cans, margarine tubs)
- potting soil
- small plastic bags

Wash the containers. Poke several small
holes in the bottom of the containers so that
the water can drain. Then fill the containers
with potting soil. Plant the seeds according
to the directions on the packet and water
them. Then place the container in a plastic
bag and tie the top. The bag will keep the
seeds moist without additional watering.
Keep the bag out of strong sunlight.

In about a week, the seeds will begin to
sprout. Remove the plastic bag and place the
container on a sunny windowsill. Be sure to

water regularly. You should also turn the container every few days so the seedlings will get sunlight on all sides. This helps the plants to grow straight.

When the sprouts have developed a second set of leaves, they are called seedlings. Before seedlings can be planted outside, they have to be "hardened off." This is a process that helps a seedling get used to the outdoors. As the weather gets warmer, place the containers outside during the day and bring them back inside at night. When it is warm enough (the back of the seed packet will tell you), the seedlings are ready to plant outside.

SEEDLINGS

Grocery stores, hardware stores, and plant nurseries sell seedlings all ready to tuck into your garden. Depending on the temperatures in your area, seedlings may need to be hardened off before they can be planted outdoors.

When planting a seedling, pack the soil firmly
around the plant.

How to Plant Seedlings
You will need:

- trowel or spoon
- soil and compost or fertilizer
- seedlings

Dig a large, deep hole that will allow plenty of room for the roots to grow. Pour compost or fertilizer into the bottom of the hole and water. Then place the seedling in the hole. Be sure to handle the seedling by its leaves (not by the stem, which can damage the plant). The seedling's bottommost leaves should be level with the ground or the soil in the container. If the hole is too deep, carefully lift the seedling and add more fertilizer. Fill in soil around the seedling and pat it down firmly. Water the area. You may also want to add a layer of mulch around outdoor plants. Mulch will keep the soil moist and warm so the plant can grow.

Repotting

At some point, you may need to repot a plant. Repotting means moving a plant to a larger pot as it grows bigger. How do you know when to repot? Lift the container and see if the roots are growing out of the holes at the bottom. If so, it's time for a bigger pot. Slip a trowel or a dull knife between the soil and the edge of the pot. Cut around the edge and then tilt the pot upside down. Tap lightly and the plant should slide out. If it doesn't, use a spoon to gently break apart the soil around the plant and ease it out. Plant as you would normally.

BULBS

A whole plant can grow from a planted bulb. Many of the early spring flowers, such as crocuses, tulips, and daf-fodils, grow from bulbs that were planted the previous fall.

You can also grow bulbs indoors and have them bloom no matter what the season. This process is called "forcing" the bulbs. Bulbs naturally rest in the ground through winter before they bloom in spring. To trick or "force" bulbs into thinking that the cold weather has come and gone, place them in the refrigerator for six to eight weeks before planting.

Tulips are beautiful flowers that grow from bulbs.

How to Plant Bulbs

You will need:

- trowel or spoon
- bulbs
- bone meal (a kind of food for bulbs)

Dig a hole about twice as deep as the bulb is tall. For most bulbs, this is from 5 to 8 inches (12–20 cm) deep. (If there is a lot of wildlife in your area, plant bulbs a little deeper to stop animals from digging them up.) Add the bone meal to the bottom of the hole and mix with the soil. Place the bulbs in the hole, pointed ends up, about 2 to 5 inches (5–12 cm) apart.

Cover them with soil and pat it down firmly. Water the area thoroughly. If your garden is outside, add a thick layer of mulch to keep the bulbs warm and moist.

Bulbs should be planted with the pointed ends up.

4
Taking Care
of Your Garden

Proper watering is essential to a healthy garden.

Your plants are busy growing, but there is still plenty of work to do to keep them healthy.

WATERING

It's important that your garden get the right amount of water. This is especially important during the summer, when the weather is usually drier and hotter. Stick your finger in the soil around the plant. If the soil is dry, it's time to water. It is best to water in late afternoon or early morning, not in the midday heat. Water at the base of the plant until the soil around it is completely moist. Be careful not to over-water your plants. A thorough watering once a week usually is enough.

FEEDING

Plant food, or fertilizer, has all of the nutrients a plant requires to stay strong and healthy. Generally, plant food is given when the plant is a seedling and again when it blooms. Don't

Regular watering is more important for container gardens than other gardens, because they can quickly dry out.

overfertilize. Read the label carefully to know how much to add. The plant food also may need to be mixed with water before it is used. For a natural alternative to fertilizer, use compost.

WEEDING

Pull weeds out while they are young, before they have a chance to develop seeds. You can buy products that kill weeds, but be careful. These weed killers often contain chemicals that you don't want to eat. Two healthy ways to prevent weeds are mulching and natural pest-proofing.

MULCHING

Mulching is a way to keep water in and weeds out. Mulch is a covering that is put on top of the soil around your plants. It blocks sunlight,

Garden Friends

Some insects and animals are good for your garden. A gardener's best friend is the earthworm. The earthworm eats through the soil and breaks it apart. The holes the worms make add air and water to the soil, which plants need to grow. As the worms eat, they leave "castings," or manure. The castings add nutrients to the soil.

Other friends in the garden are ladybugs, spiders, and lacewings. Frogs and toads, bats, snakes, skunks, and praying mantises are also helpful. They all eat harmful insects. Bees help your garden grow by pollinating your plants' flowers.

which keeps weeds from growing. Mulch also holds in moisture and keeps the soil warm when the weather is cool, and cool when the weather is hot. The best time to mulch is after a good rain. Don't forget to weed first!

You can make your own mulch by using damp newspaper or cardboard. Place it around the plant and use rocks to weigh it down. You can also make mulch with sheets of black plastic. Black plastic is easy to find—you can buy rolls of it at a garden center or just cut up garbage bags. Weigh the bags down with rocks or bricks.

PEST-PROOFING

Garden pests include aphids, cucumber beetles, flea beetles, snails, and slugs. Keep these pests out by using natural methods instead of harmful chemicals. For an outdoor garden, plant herbs and flowers that will repel (keep away) insects. Marigolds, sweet

Snails are pests that can destroy your garden.

basil, lavender, and mint are good bug repel-
lents. Planting radishes with cucumbers will
help control cucumber beetles.

For an indoor garden, spray your plants with
soapy water. Brush off the insects with a cotton
swab. You can also make your own bug spray to
use indoors or out. Blend onion, garlic, or hot
pepper with some water. Strain the garlic, fill
your sprayer with the water, and spritz your
plants. The smell will keep the bugs away.

Chemicals and Your Garden

Chemical fertilizers and pesticide (insect poison) sprays are commonly used in gardening. Yet people often aren't aware of the dangers that chemicals pose to themselves and their environment. Here are some reasons you may choose not to use chemicals in your garden:

• Soil that is chemically fertilized loses its life over time and is no longer good for gardening.

• Insects may be pests, but chemical sprays kill off helpful insects as well as harmful ones. After awhile, pests learn how to resist pesticides anyway.

• Chemical fertilizers and sprays can miss their targets, landing in our drinking water, oceans, and in the air. This poses a danger to humans, animals, and the environment.

• Pesticides can remain on your fruits or vegetables, making them dangerous to eat.

You don't need to spend a lot of money to grow a garden. You don't even need a backyard! A small plot of land, a flowerpot, or even a milk jug can be the start of any kind of garden. It can be full of vegetables, herbs, flowers, or whatever you want to grow. Your garden can be indoors or outdoors, on a porch, a windowsill, or a roof. It can be big or small, square or round—use your imagination!

SAFETY TIPS

Gardening is hard work, especially when you're first getting started. Stay safe by doing the following:

- When digging, keep your back straight and use your legs for power.
- When lifting, weeding, or planting, bend with your knees and lift with your legs, not with your back.
- Wear sunscreen if you're working outside, even in cold weather or on cloudy days.
- Take regular breaks so you don't get too tired.
- Drink plenty of water or fruit juice, especially on hot days.
- Don't leave tools lying around where they can be stepped on.

Remember, chemical fertilizers and pesticides are poisons. They need to be handled carefully at all times.

• Read the label and follow the directions. Don't add more of the product than is absolutely necessary.
• Many fertilizers and pesticides come in a powder form and need to be mixed with water. Mix outside, in an area protected from the wind.
• Don't breathe the product.
• Don't eat or smoke while handling chemical products. Wash your hands with soap and water immediately after you've finished.
• Keep the products away from children and pets.
• When the container is empty, wrap it in newspaper and put in the garbage. Never reuse the containers.

NEW WORDS

annual a plant that lives for only one season

biennial a plant that lives for only two seasons

bone meal crushed animal bone used as a fertilizer for bulbs

botanical garden a large garden open to the public where plants are grown and studied

bulb a large, swollen underground seed from which plants grow

casting manure, such as worm droppings

container garden an indoor or outdoor garden that is grown in containers

compost decayed plant scraps used to feed plants and soil

fertilizer plant food

garden plot an outdoor garden in the ground

harden off to get a seedling used to the outdoors before putting it in the ground

herb a plant that is used for medicine and seasoning

mulch a material used to protect a plant's roots from heat or cold and to keep soil moist

nursery a gardening center where plants are grown and sold

nutrient a substance needed by living things to grow

peat moss decayed moss used to keep soil moist and warm

perennial a plant that comes back year after year

pollinate to carry pollen to a plant to fertilize it

repellent a substance that keeps something away, such as insects

seed the part of a plant that grows to become a new plant

seedling a young, small plant

spade a tool with a flat blade used for digging

spread total width of a full-grown plant

trench a narrow ditch

trowel a handheld spade used for digging

vermiculite a light rock that absorbs water to give plants moisture

FOR FURTHER READING

Bradley, Fern Marshall and Barbara W. Ellis. *Rodale's All New Encyclopedia of Organic Gardening*. Emmaus, PA: Rodale Press, 1992.

Brown, Marc T. *Your First Garden Book*. New York: Little, Brown & Company, 1981.

Marken, Bill. *Annuals for Dummies*. Indianapolis: IDG Books Worldwide, 1998.

Verey, Rosemary. *The Herb Growing Book*. Boston: Little, Brown & Company, 1980.

Williams, Carol. *Bringing A Garden to Life*. New York: Bantam Books, 1998.

RESOURCES

The American Community Gardening Association
100 N. 20th Street, 5th floor
Philadelphia, PA 19103
Web site: *www.communitygarden.org*
215-988-8785
Supports community gardens in urban and rural locations. Lists many regional community gardens.

Garden Net
www.gardennet.com
A good, all-purpose source of gardening information. Has many links to other garden Web sites.

National Gardening Association
180 Flynn Avenue
Burlington, VT 05401
802-863-1308
Web site: *www.garden.org*
Offers good gardening tips, publishes *National Gardening Magazine*, has youth programs.

Gardening Companies

These companies will send you a free catalog if you write, call, or visit their Web sites:

W. Atlee Burpee Company
300 Park Avenue
Warminster, PA 18974
800-333-5808
Web site: *www.burpee.com*

Park Seed
1 Parkton Avenue
Greenwood, SC 29647
800-275-9941
Web site: *www.parkseed.com*

INDEX

About the Author
Ruth Chasek lives in Brooklyn, New York with her husband and two children. She works as an editor at a publishing company.